321.5 Brennan
What is an oligarchy?

Property of: Mentor Public Library
8215 Mentor Ave.
Mentor, OH 44060   06/07/2013

WHAT IS AN
OLIGARCHY?

JOSEPH BRENNAN

Crabtree Publishing Company
www.crabtreebooks.com

Crabtree Publishing Company

www.crabtreebooks.com

Produced and developed by Netscribes Inc.

Author: Joseph Brennan
Publishing plan research and development:
 Sean Charlebois, Reagan Miller
 Crabtree Publishing Company
Editors: Valerie J. Weber, Lynn Peppas
Proofreaders: Wendy Scavuzzo, Sarah Chasse
Art director: Dibakar Acharjee
Picture researcher: Sandeep Kumar Guthikonda
Project coordinator: Kathy Middleton
Print coordinator: Katherine Berti
Production coordinator: Kenneth J. Wright
Prepress technician: Kenneth J. Wright
Cover design: Margaret Amy Salter, Katherine Berti

Front cover: Statue of Leonidas at Sparta city in Greece (left); Shack housing in South Africa (background); Portrait of Maximilien de Robespierre (1758-1794) (inset bottom); Yegor Gaidar of Russia in 2008 (inset top)

Title Page: An Occupy Wall Street protester, September 17, 2012, on the one year anniversary of the movement in New York.

Photographs:
Title page: STAN HONDA/AFP/GettyImages; P4: Lintao Zhang/Getty Images; P5: Leemage/Gettyimages; P6: fivepointsix/Shutterstock; P7: FPG/Hulton Archive/Getty Images; P8-9: Mart/Shutterstock; P10: Kzenon/Shutterstock; P11: Leemage/Gettyimages; P12: French School/Gettyimages; P13: DEA / L. PEDICINI/Getty Images; P14: Ifelix/Shutterstock; P15: kai hecker / Shutterstock; P16: Ted Spiegel/CORBIS; P17: Maya Vidon/AFP Photo/Getty Images; P18: DEA / A. DAGLI ORTI/De Agostini/Getty Images; P19: Three Lions/Getty Images; P20: CORBIS; P21: Bettmann/CORBIS; P22: Antonio Gisbert/The Bridgeman/Gettyimages; P23: Bettmann/CORBIS; P24: Corbis; P25: Yao Dawei/Xinhua Press/Corbis; P26:Photos.com/ Thinkstock; P27: The Print Collector/Corbis; P28: William Aiken Walker/The Bridgeman Art Library/Getty Images; P29: French Ministry of Defence/dpa/Corbis; P30: Jeff Greenberg/Gettyimages; P31: Claudio Divizia/Shutterstock; P32: Bettmann/CORBIS; P33: Keystone-France/Gamma-Keystone via Getty Images; P34: Mike Tan C. T./Shutterstock; P35: BartlomiejMagierowski / Shutterstock; P36: Stuart Miles/Shutterstock; P37: Peter Scholz / Shutterstock; P40: Martin Rose/Getty Images; P41: DeAgostini/Getty Images; P42: Mohamed Elsayyed / Shutterstock; P43: Sergio Goya/dpa/Corbis; P44: ALEXANDER JOE/AFP/Getty Images; P45: Nick Pavlakis/Shutterstock. Shutterstock: front cover (left); Thinkstock: front cover (background); Wikimedia Commons/Jurg Vollmer/Maiakinfo: front cover (inset top); Wikimedia Commons/Carnavalet Museum: front cover (inset bottom)

Library and Archives Canada Cataloguing in Publication

Brennan, Joseph K. (Joseph Killorin)
 What is an oligarchy? / Joseph Killorin Brennan.

(Forms of government)
Includes index.
Issued also in electronic format.
ISBN 978-0-7787-5320-9 (bound).--ISBN 978-0-7787-5327-8 (pbk.)

 1. Oligarchy--Juvenile literature. I. Title. II. Series: Forms of government (St. Catharines, Ont.)

JC419.B74 2013   j321'.5   C2013-901027-0

Library of Congress Cataloging-in-Publication Data

CIP available at Library of Congress

Crabtree Publishing Company

www.crabtreebooks.com   1-800-387-7650

Printed in the U.S.A./042013/SX20130306

Copyright © **2013 CRABTREE PUBLISHING COMPANY.** All rights reserved. No part of this publication may be reproduced, stored in a retrieval system or be transmitted in any form or by any means, electronic, mechanical, photocopying, recording, or otherwise, without the prior written permission of Crabtree Publishing Company.

Published in Canada
Crabtree Publishing
616 Welland Ave.
St. Catharines, Ontario
L2M 5V6

Published in the United States
Crabtree Publishing
PMB 59051
350 Fifth Avenue, 59th Floor
New York, New York 10118

Published in the United Kingdom
Crabtree Publishing
Maritime House
Basin Road North, Hove
BN41 1WR

Published in Australia
Crabtree Publishing
3 Charles Street
Coburg North
VIC 3058

CONTENTS

A Secret Government

A national government is a group of people in charge of ruling or managing a country. The kind of government determines who is in charge. Not all governments are the same. Some governments are democracies, **theocracies**, **monarchies**, or **dictatorships**.

In 2013, Xi Jinping is expected to become the head of China's government. He represents a small group of insiders. These oligarchs control much of the country and have become extremely wealthy as a result.

Oligarchy: Rule of the Few

An oligarchy is usually a secret form of government. Most oligarchies will hide the fact that they hold power. The term *oligarchy* is made up of two Greek words. *Oligos* means "a few." *Archo* means "to rule or to command." Together, they mean a government by a small group of people.

In ancient Greece, the people did not want one ruler. They actually elected their oligarchy. But very few countries throughout history wanted an oligarchy. Over time, the definition of oligarchy changed slightly to mean a few powerful people controlling a country. Rarely were they elected.

Types of Oligarchies

Oligarchies have taken many forms. They often hide behind some other type of government. Some democracies appear to elect their leaders. But their true leaders are hidden. Other oligarchies are a group of families. These **aristocrats** can hide behind a type of government called a monarchy. Other oligarchies are the wealthiest people in a country. This type of government is also called a **plutocracy**. And some oligarchies are made up of the rich and of those related by birth. These features make them the most popular and **elite** in their society.

All these types of oligarchies have existed at different times throughout history. Many still exist today.

The Grand Council of Venice was a group of oligarchs who ruled openly.

How to Identify an Oligarchy

There is an easy way to discover a secret elite. Look for those people who have what everyone else wants. Money, land, and valuable things bring power. Anyone who controls the food supply has power. Someone who has all the oil or water or wheat has power. Someone who commands an army or a secret police force can control a whole country.

That person does not have to openly take charge. He or she does not have to say, "I rule this country." The people with the real power can make secret agreements with others. They can find people who want what they want. They can make sure that they and their friends will get the good things first. Their friends will be happy. Their needs will always be met. An oligarchy is a small group of citizens who get what they want.

Why Is an Oligarchy Secret?

Many oligarchies hide behind a king or a **dictator**. This ruler claims to be in charge. But in reality, a small group of powerful people may really be in control. The oligarchy stays hidden. That way, it cannot be blamed if something goes wrong.

AN OBVIOUS OLIGARCHY

One type of oligarchy cannot be hidden. A small group of people of one race can rule by force. They control the larger population of other races.

The South African Oligarchy

Millions of Africans lived in South Africa. In 1652, Holland established a colony there. Great Britain later took over. At first, Europeans lived and worked side by side with Africans. Anyone could own property. The situation soon changed.

Huge diamond deposits were found in 1867. Gold was discovered in 1886. The Europeans needed many workers for the mines and farms. Yet they only wanted to pay low wages. Africans were also growing food on successful farms. Their success drove down the prices for European farmers.

So the government passed the Natives' Land Act of 1913. It stated that the Europeans would own 87 percent of the land. Yet they were only 20 percent of the population. The law also controlled the members of the two largest tribes of Africans. They were forced to live together on land **reserves**, called the African Homelands.

Under whites-only rule, millions of native Africans were forced to live on small tracts of land called townships. These poor townships continue to house South Africans today.

Thousands of Africans were forced into unsafe gold or diamond mines to work. By law, only whites could be bosses.

Effects of the Natives' Land Act

African farmers were put out of business. They had to work for European farmers. The homelands were too small to farm, and too many people were forced to live there. Very few Africans could earn a living there. They had no choice but to work for Europeans. Most worked in the mines. They were paid very little for this hard and dangerous work. Africans became very poor, while Europeans became very rich.

Apartheid

South Africa established a policy called *apartheid*. This word means "separate." Laws did not allow Africans to work certain jobs. Almost every well-paid job was given to whites. Africans were not allowed to be educated or hired for jobs that used their abilities.

By the 1980s, South Africa had a huge police force to keep power. Riots and deadly violence got worse. Finally apartheid ended in 1994.

Mandela and Apartheid's End

A young African lawyer named Nelson Mandela was imprisoned for decades for trying to end apartheid. Other countries felt that this was wrong. They stopped investing in South African businesses. The country and its policies about Africans had to change. Starting in the 1980s, laws were rewritten, allowing Africans more rights. They could vote again. Mandela was freed from prison in 1990 and elected president in 1994.

A surprisingly high number of oligarchs live in Scandinavia, which includes the countries of Norway, Sweden, and Denmark. They benefit from a strong elected government.

Venice, **city-state** of traders, had one of the wealthiest oligarchies during the 1300s and 1400s. It was a city filled with billionaires.

Power oligarchies ruled Rome when it controlled much of Europe, northern Africa, and southwestern Asia from 135 BCE to 285 CE. They fought with each other for great wealth.

The **descendants** of the Spanish conquerors still rule Guatemala. They have used their people to provide cheap labor throughout their history.

Voters in Argentina have re-elected the same oligarchs for three centuries. The people there do not choose change because they are afraid of what would happen next.

Oligarchies have controlled Egypt for decades. Even the recent overthrow of the government has not broken their hold on the country.

U.S.

Canada

States

Mexico

Bahamas

Cuba
Dominican Republic
Jamaica
Haiti
Belize
Guatemala
Honduras
El Salvador
Nicaragua
Costa Rica
Panama
Caribbean Sea

Venezuela
Colombia
Ecuador
Peru
Brazil
Bolivia
Chile
Paraguay
Argentina
Uruguay

Labrador Sea

ARCTIC OCEAN

Iceland
Reykjavík

Ireland
United Kingdom

France

NORTH ATLANTIC OCEAN

Portugal
Spain

Morocco

Algeria

Western Sahara
Mauritania
Mali
Senegal
Gambia
Guinea-Bissau
Guinea
Sierra Leone
Liberia
Côte d'Ivoire
Ghana
Burkina Faso
Benin

SOUTH ATLANTIC OCEAN

SOUTHERN OCEAN

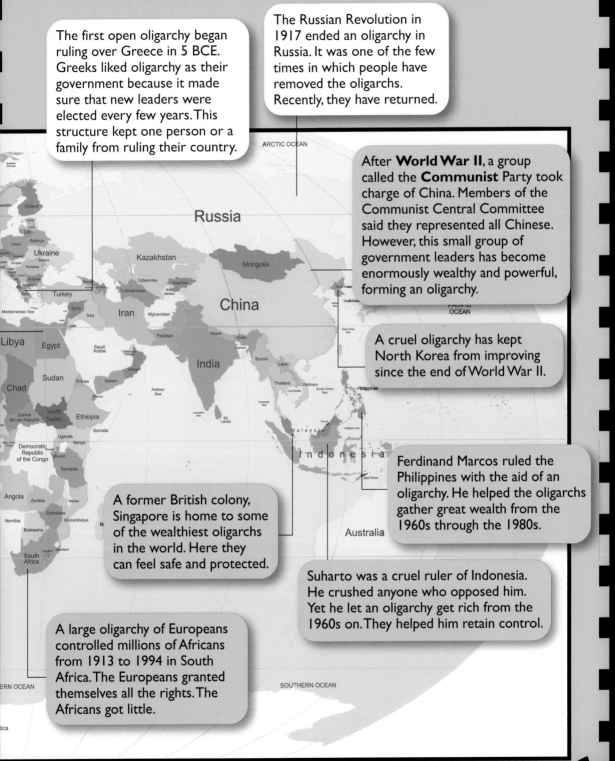

The first open oligarchy began ruling over Greece in 5 BCE. Greeks liked oligarchy as their government because it made sure that new leaders were elected every few years. This structure kept one person or a family from ruling their country.

The Russian Revolution in 1917 ended an oligarchy in Russia. It was one of the few times in which people have removed the oligarchs. Recently, they have returned.

After **World War II**, a group called the **Communist** Party took charge of China. Members of the Communist Central Committee said they represented all Chinese. However, this small group of government leaders has become enormously wealthy and powerful, forming an oligarchy.

A cruel oligarchy has kept North Korea from improving since the end of World War II.

A former British colony, Singapore is home to some of the wealthiest oligarchs in the world. Here they can feel safe and protected.

Ferdinand Marcos ruled the Philippines with the aid of an oligarchy. He helped the oligarchs gather great wealth from the 1960s through the 1980s.

Suharto was a cruel ruler of Indonesia. He crushed anyone who opposed him. Yet he let an oligarchy get rich from the 1960s on. They helped him retain control.

A large oligarchy of Europeans controlled millions of Africans from 1913 to 1994 in South Africa. The Europeans granted themselves all the rights. The Africans got little.

ORIGINS OF OLIGARCHY

A class of schoolchildren provides a good example of how oligarchies work. Usually, there are various groups of friends. Yet one group seems to be more powerful. They are the group everyone else wants to join. They might be the most popular. They could be the best dressed. They might also be the best athletes. No one elected them the leaders. Still, they are. They decide what is cool. The rest of the class follows. They have control over other kids. They might be pretty or handsome. They are often fast talkers, funny, or mean. Their power can come from a wide variety sources.

Early Oligarchies

Humans first began to gather as groups in prehistoric times. These groups became tribes or small societies made up of families. A leader took charge. This person could be a chief. Groups of elders or warriors could also make the decisions for the group. These few told the others what to do. They were the first oligarchs.

Oligarchies and Farming

Around 3100 BCE, the first societies claimed land. They planted crops and dug ditches to bring water. A village was built. Related families called clans looked after that land. A chief or **warlord** controlled the clans. Certain families and clans became oligarchies.

The roots of oligarchy are seen even in a schoolyard, where a few kids tend to have power over the larger group.

Herds of cattle allowed individuals to gather great wealth. With their wealth, cattle owners gained power in society.

Their land had to be defended or others might come and take away their hard work. In time, they even decided to attack others. They took over their neighbors' lands, bringing in more wealth. In this way, the oligarchs grew richer than the others.

Another big change came over time. People began raising cattle around 2300 BCE. Clans gathered large herds. They could take this wealth with them wherever they went. Humans also gathered sheep, cattle, and goats. Societies grew larger. They formed huge armies. Wars were fought to gain and to protect wealth. The oligarchies used their armies to take land, food, money, and slaves from others. They also had to protect what they had from others.

Cattle Means Wealth

Many words for money come from words for cattle. The word, **capital**, comes from the Latin word *caput,* or a head of cattle. The Norse word *fe* means both "wealth" and "cattle." It also gives us *fee*. It was combined with the Celtic word *od*, which means "land." *Fee-od* became *feudal*. In a **feudal system**, most of the people worked for a leader. The leader and his oligarchy became wealthy. The workers stayed poor.

3100 BCE	The first human societies claimed land
2300 BCE	Humans began raising cattle

ANCIENT OLIGARCHIES

At various times in their history, ancient Greece and Rome had oligarchies. These were some of the first and best-known oligarchies. Yet in both **empires**, they operated differently.

Greek Oligarchy

Ancient Greece was not one country. The Greeks lived in city-states, such as Athens and Sparta. At times, kings, dictators, and democracies ruled these city-states. But around 5 BCE, various city-states used a form of democracy that became an oligarchy. Only those who had land or money were expected to help govern.

The Greeks thought it was a good idea to keep the same people from being in charge all the time. Judges and government officials only served in one post for a short time. The way they were elected to office made sure no one cheated. Groups of men drew straws to pick their leaders. Whoever picked the longest straw was chosen.

This may sound very fair but it was not. Not everyone could vote. About 300,000 people lived in Athens, but only the 38,000 landowners and wealthy individuals in Greece could vote. And most of the land and wealth was concentrated in the hands of only 1,200 men. They were worth the **equivalent** of $1 million each in today's dollars. Most people were poor and powerless.

Merchants gained great wealth in the marketplace. Greeks with money or land could be a part of the oligarchy.

The Rule of the Few in Rome

In the 500s BCE, Romans overthrew their king and started a republic. In a republic, citizens and the leaders they elected held the power. They formed a government. But again, only a few people in Rome gained real power. When Rome began conquering other countries, a select group of its generals became powerful dictators.

Still, the Romans liked to pretend that all citizens were equal in their republic. In reality, most of the ruling **class** were worth about $4 million each by today's standards. Julius Caesar and other generals were nearly billionaires. They ruled almost 60 million people who paid them taxes. Rome became the model that other conquerors followed. Oligarchies of the military and superwealthy soon ruled empires throughout history.

A Roman general, Gaius Marius gained great popularity with his troops. His victories in war brought him acclaim from Romans as well. This political support made him part of the ruling class.

Aristotle's Definitions

Aristotle was a Greek philosopher born in 384 BCE. He defined different types of government. The Rule of One was that of a king. The Rule of Few meant a royal family was in power. Rule of Many was democracy. Aristotle attached a value to these types of government. For example, a tyrant or dictator is a bad king. An oligarchy is a bad royal family. A mob is a bad democracy.

pre-400 BCE–300s CE	Greek oligarchies rule
135 BCE–285 CE	Roman oligarchies

PERFECT OLIGARCHIES

The glory of the Roman and Greek empires ended by 500 CE. Most of the world seemed to go backward. Small groups fought each other for control. Warlords and tribes ruled. Kings controlled small areas, while their knights fought for power. The common people worked like slaves on farms that the wealthy owned. Without order in most places, oligarchies needed protection.

Merchant oligarchs helped fund building Saint Mark's cathedral.

Italy's City-States

The Italian city-states were governed by oligarchies. The city-states of Florence, Siena, and Venice were very successful. They were nearly perfect oligarchies. These cities held little land. Many citizens were merchants or traders. They moved goods on ships in the Mediterranean Sea. Without land to inherit, the elite gathered wealth. They elected leaders but kept them powerless. The real power was concentrated in groups that formed the oligarchy. In Venice, the oligarchic leadership was called the Great Council. In Siena, those who ruled were called the Oligarchy of Nine. In 1287, this group ruled in a unique way.

Its members were not the richest men in the city. They were the upper classes, the bankers, and merchant classes. They were linked together by a few families related through marriage.

The real oligarchs had much greater wealth. Yet these super rich allowed these poorer elites to rule. This special arrangement kept the most powerful few from fighting among themselves. Though the Oligarchy of Nine actually ran the government, the super rich were allowed to do what they wanted. They just could not take over the government.

The Beauty of Florence

In Florence, the powerful businessmen and merchants kept the very wealthy and the common people out of their government. The merchant **guilds** became powerful. Together with the wealthiest families, they got rich in banking and the wool industry. The Medici family and other members of the oligarchy paid the greatest artists of the **Renaissance** to work for them. They made the city into a showplace of their power.

Oligarchies Produced Great Art

Ruler and statesman Lorenzo de' Medici supported and paid the greatest artists of the Renaissance. Michelangelo, Leonardo da Vinci, and Sandro Botticelli created fantastic works. The guilds built the magnificent Duomo, the domed cathedral of Santa Maria del Fiore. Paid for by Franciso de' Medici, the Uffizi museum contains some of Italy's greatest artwork. Elaborate bridges and fountains decorate the city. The wealth of the oligarchies remains on full display in Florence today.

Leonardo da Vinci's well-known *Mona Lisa* was one of the great works of art that wealthy Italian oligarchs sponsored.

810—1500	Venice ruled by oligarchies
late 1000—1555	Siena ruled by oligarchies including the Oligarchy of Nine

OLIGARCHIES CHANGE

Oligarchies are constantly changing to suit their times and governments. Wealthy citizens may form them to keep a **corrupt** king from taking their money. If an elected government is weak and cannot keep the population under control, the oligarchies could lose everything. They want to bring calm and peace to a society. This situation allows the wealthy to keep their riches and make more money.

An oligarchy has to make sure that the government has firm control of the people, but not of the oligarchy itself. This is why a group such as the Nine in Siena was created. It becomes the official government, while the real power is still held by the few. The few use their money to make sure everyone does what they want.

Marcos Rules the Philippines

Oligarchies have long controlled Indonesia and the Philippines. Each oligarchy has a different kind of changing power structure. In the Spanish American War in 1898, the United States conquered the Philippines. Wealthy local merchants took charge of the colony that the U.S. had set up.

In 1965, Ferdinand Marcos became president. He was from the merchant class. The oligarchy continued to operate invisibly behind him. There was a constant struggle between Marcos and the wealthy people he represented. He was supposed to do what they wanted him to do. Many of the oligarchs had their own armies. They used them to defend their wealth. Marcos had the country's army to keep the oligarchy in check. He controlled the country and kept the oligarchs happy.

Ferdinand Marcos ruled the Philippines as a dictator. He also controlled a group of oligarchs who helped him to maintain power for decades.

Indonesian dictator Suharto gave his country's great wealth to a small group of businessmen. In turn, they helped his family become very, very rich.

Suharto Helps the Oligarchs

In Indonesia, Suharto took power differently. A military general, he took control of the country's government in 1966. Then he allowed a group of oligarchs who were foreign businessmen to gain great wealth. Suharto used the wealth of his oligarchs. They paid poor people to riot, creating fake street protests. Stopping the protests allowed Suharto to take total control of the county. He said he needed complete power to make the country calm again. Suharto killed or tortured anyone who tried to stop him. Terror kept the people from stopping him. It also protected the oligarchs.

Passing Down Wealth

In the 1980s, Suharto's adult children began to take over parts of the oligarchy, going after the country's new oil wealth. Their fortunes grew to $16 billion. They owned as much land as the country of Belgium. His children brought in their own foreign businesses. These companies replaced their father's old oligarchies. Their father protected their businesses. Soon the children were fighting each other.

AN OLIGARCHY'S CITIZENS

Rarely are outsiders invited to join an oligarchy. Having more people dilutes the power of the oligarchy. In the city-state of Venice, however, people were actually asked to join the rulers. It helped everyone make money.

Venice had a unique way of providing money for trading. Its merchants had to take long and expensive voyages. To raise money, they used a *commenda*. This type of contract had two partners. A wealthy member of the oligarchy put up the money. An ordinary citizen took the risk of travelling aboard the ship to make sure the voyage was successful.

This arrangement allowed common people to join the city's elite. The Great Council was a group of oligarchs. Every year, they allowed the outsiders to join. This growth brought in new ideas and fresh energy. Over time, the *commenda* ended. The state took over all trade. Only the oligarchy profited from it. Soon Venice's success was over. By not bringing in outsiders, the oligarchy ruined Venice.

The great wealth of the city-state of Venice was based partly on its successful shipping industry. A group of billionaires acted as an oligarchy to build a grand city.

Venice and the *Commenda*

In 1330, Venice had more than 100,000 people. They lived in a very small but very wealthy city.

Venice—a City of Billionaires

Venice was once filled with billionaires. One out of every 400 people was super rich, so Venice protected its oligarchy. The General Assembly was a gathering of the citizens of Venice. They had the power to veto or reject any laws they disagreed with. Yet they never did. The government even built ships for the wealthy. No one disagreed.

The poor coffee plantation workers in Guatemala lived in shacks with dirt floors. The wealthy plantation owners owned huge, fancy houses called haciendas.

Forcing the People To Work

In some countries, such as Guatemala, the oligarchies harmed the people. They took away the rights of ordinary citizens. The Guatemalan oligarchy began in the 1500s. Spanish **conquistadors** invaded South America. The descendants of these soldiers have ruled the country for more than 500 years and are still ruling today. Twenty-two families have controlled all the politics. They use a merchant guild similar to Florence's guilds during the Renaissance. However, this guild harmed the country.

The guild controlled all trade and taxes. Not much changed for 300 years. Then in the 1800s, coffee became popular. The guild passed laws taking most of the land and turning it over to coffee farms. They began to produce large profits. They also created a forced labor system. Everyone had to prove they had a job and were forced to work. They got very low wages on the coffee farms. The oligarchy misused their people.

THE PEOPLE'S OLIGARCHIES

Sometimes powerful local people form their own oligarchies when a government lacks power. In Italy in the mid-1900s, local leaders formed the Mafia. This oligarchy uses violence to control certain areas. Mafia families have fought the government and each other for centuries to protect their power. Many operate like warlords in feudal states. They conduct illegal activities. Everyone is afraid to challenge them. If police or judges try to stop them, they are often murdered. The Mafia does not openly rule. Yet its secret power is known to everyone.

The Mafia in the United States

During the 1800s, large numbers of Italian immigrants moved to the United States. They settled in the poorest areas of the big cities. The government did not function in these slums. The new immigrants often needed protection from other residents. Local police and officials also took advantage of those who could not speak English. The Mafia came along with the Italian immigrants. It became the real authority in some places. As an oligarchy, it remained a secret power group. Similar groups protected immigrants from other countries as well.

Although they were illegal, these oligarchies succeeded. They provided a source of wealth through criminal activities. They also protected immigrant businesses from other criminals.

Governments have tried to control the Mafia. Even forcing its leaders to testify in the U.S. Congress has not stopped this organization.

The Hatfield-McCoy feud continued into the mid-1900s. In 1959, a 12-year-old boy and his 76-year-old grandfather were arrested. They supposedly shot three members of a Hatfield family in a fight over rights to land.

Feuds in the Mountains

Oligarchies also formed in the Appalachian Mountains of Kentucky and West Virginia in the 1880s. **Feuds** between local wealthy and powerful families began. The most famous of these feuds were between the Hatfields and the McCoys. At first, unfair elections were the basis for these disputes. The families also fought over valuable mining claims. Later they battled for control of illegal criminal activities.

The Hatfields owned a large area of land with a fortune in timber on it. Their clan included doctors, lawyers, a governor, and a senator. They were leaders of the Democratic Party in West Virginia. Their increasing wealth and power threatened other local oligarchs. Outsiders had come into eastern Kentucky to obtain mineral and timber wealth. They used the local McCoy family to attempt to compete with the Hatfields' power.

Oligarchies Do Battle

The Clay County Wars in Kentucky were a series of feuds that lasted from 1839 to 1901. Two wealthy and politically powerful families fought over land and salt-manufacturing operations. Coal, railroads, and timber were also at stake. The war grew intense. People from other families were at risk. Both families hired armies of soldiers with their own money. They also had armies of lawyers to sue each other. Over time, the violence died down with neither side winning.

STRUGGLES WITHIN

Members of an oligarchy may not agree with each other. In Siena and Indonesia, different forces within an oligarchy struggled to gain control. In Rome, competing oligarchies fought each other. This is the natural result of powerful people trying to control other powerful people.

The Puritans were an oligarchy with strict religious rules. They controlled the young colony. But the Puritans fought among themselves. To be a member of the oligarchy, each colonist had to join the local Protestant church. But the oligarchy kept out anyone who they did not want. They even forced members of the oligarchy to leave the colony.

Only members of the oligarchy were allowed to vote and participate in the colony's government. The Puritans were criticized for denying so many people places in their new society. They said they wanted to keep the colony strong. They even discouraged other people from moving into the community. Eventually, their oligarchy acted just like the English who had attacked them back home.

Kicking the Oligarchs Out

The Puritans were members of a religious group in England. They had been attacked there for their religious beliefs. The king granted them land in North America. In 1613, they sailed from England and founded the Massachusetts Bay Colony at Plymouth.

Two hundred years after the Puritans arrived in North America, they began to be called the Pilgrims. Often oligarchies, such as the leaders of the Puritans, are divided, and members quarrel or rebel.

People came to North America to practice their own religion. However, some people, such as Anne Hutchinson, were forced to start new colonies to practice what they believed.

Settling New Places

Roger Williams was part of the Puritan oligarchy. He was thrown out of the Massachusetts Bay Colony and moved to present-day Rhode Island. There he founded his own colony. Anne Hutchinson was also expelled from the colony. She moved to present-day New York. There she could follow her religious beliefs. The Puritans' oligarchy helped to create new colonies in different areas.

The Iron Law of Oligarchy

In 1911, an Italian scientist named Robert Michels developed a theory that explained how oligarchies work. He argued that inside any group, certain things always happen. The people who have power want to keep it. So, to stay in power, these leaders do things that are not good for the group. They might waste money. They may ignore good advice. As long they keep their power, no one can blame them for these mistakes. This is how many oligarchies fail at governing others.

WHO RULES?

Oligarchies can form even when the people overthrow an evil ruler. These oligarchies come into power while pretending to be a government of the people. The more powerful they become, the more they become evil rulers themselves.

Russia Creates a New Oligarchy

One of the poorest countries in Europe, Russia had remained the same for hundreds of years. Most people in the countryside worked like slaves on the land. The **Bolshevik** Revolution shook Russia in 1917. In a rare event, people rose up against the oligarchs. A group called the Communist Party replaced those in power. At first, the world saw an amazing change.

Trading Oligarchies

The Communists vowed to change the country and its poverty. They formed a central committee. This oligarchy took total control of every business in the country. It soon produced all kinds of modern goods. Sadly, their success in the factories was not repeated down on the farm. Russia could not produce enough food for its people. People began to starve. Much of the wealth of the state went to the military or the Communist Party leaders, who lived comfortably.

Russian posters promoted the overthrow of the oligarchs by the people. However, those oligarchs were simply replaced by another small group of insiders who ran the country.

As part of an oligarchy, Kim Jong II (far right) ran North Korea from 1994 until 2011. He had inherited his position from his father, Kim II-Sung. He passed the leadership to his son Kim Jong-Un (second from right).

North Korean Oligarchy

North Korea went through a similar situation after World War II ended in 1945. Korea was divided at the war's finish. Communists took over North Korea. A small group of oligarchs formed a Central Committee like the one in Russia. They controlled every part of the economy.

In South Korea, citizens enjoy a modern life. In contrast, North Korea does not have enough food and few books or computers. The Communist Party stops any contact with the outside world. Like in Russia, only the few that control the Communist Party live a modern life. The rest of the country is a backward place where time has nearly stopped. At night, North Korea is nearly dark. The state cannot even provide enough electricity.

Preventing Oligarchs

In the 1400s, the Ming Dynasty ruled China. They decided to build a huge **fleet** to sail around much of the world. It showed off China's wealth. But the Chinese were not trying to trade or conquer new worlds. The Chinese did not want wealthy merchants in their country. So they burned their fleet. They closed their doors to the outside world. Their traders would never get rich. They would never form an oligarchy that might threaten the emperors and their families.

OLIGARCHY TO DEMOCRACY

An oligarchy does not hold elections or vote on who has the most power. It often works behind the scenes. Among the powerful, control is not given away. It is taken. However, at times, the struggle for control in a country can be surprising. A group of oligarchs can change the course of history.

Many of the first oligarchies were formed to protect the wealthy from kings who tried to take their land and property. English barons forced King John to give up some of his power.

Controlling a King

In 1215, King John of England was a weak leader who misused his powers. Below him was a group of **barons**, who formed an oligarchy. They controlled the best lands in the country. They also had their own armies. The barons all agreed with each other and united to stand up to John.

They forced King John to sign the Magna Carta. This document limited the powers of the king. He could not throw the barons in jail. He could not tax them too much. It also provided for a council of 25 barons. They would make sure the king obeyed. If he did not, civil war would break out.

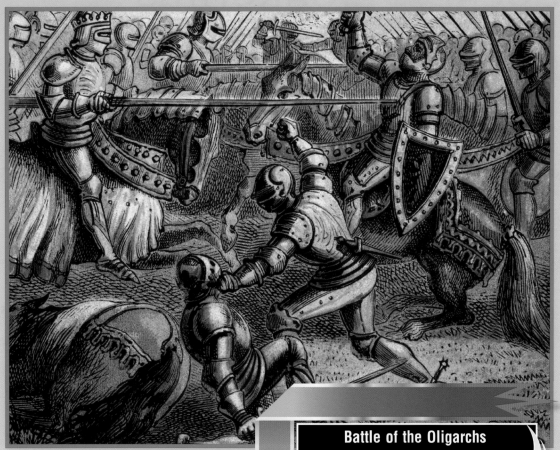

In the 1400s, two different families of oligarchs fought the War of the Roses for control of country. The white rose and red rose were symbols for each group.

A New Part of Government

In 1265, England elected its first **Parliament**. This body of men represented different parts of the country. The king was still powerful, but some major changes were coming. This Parliament was a new oligarchy. It had knights and wealthy aristocrats. Yet it also had members who were wealthy farmers and people from different parts of the country. The variety of members made it strong. It stood up to the king. In the end, it ruled the country.

Battle of the Oligarchs

After the Magna Carta, there was a struggle between two groups of elites. Two families, the House of Lancaster and the House of York, wanted to be the next line of kings. Lancaster won. It changed England into a **bureaucracy**. This government stays the same no matter who is in charge. This large central government helped the elites keep the king's powers in check. In the end, it led to Parliament ruling the country. After that, kings had no real powers.

LOCAL OLIGARCHIES

Oligarchies often begin when no other authority is in place. An oligarchy can completely take over a small country, particularly if it is an island. No outside authority can challenge it. The island of Barbados was taken over by England in the mid-1600s. In 1680, about 60,000 people were living there. More than 39,000 slaves worked its huge sugar plantations. Two-thirds of the people were controlled by the other third.

The Rule of 175

Only 175 men owned the sugar plantations on Barbados. They made up the government, including the judges and the officials. These 175 men allowed each other to do whatever they wanted. The rest of the island, slaves and colonists, had no rights and no way to improve their lives.

This situation also existed in the southern colonies of America from the 1600s to the mid-1800s. Planters raised cotton and tobacco on huge plantations. Slaves did most of the work, but only the planters had power or rights. They became an elite group and ruled the weak local governments. As a result, the South did not change. It built few factories or railroads. The North was much more wealthy and developed.

On the plantations of the American South, a few wealthy landowners were oligarchs. They controlled poor whites and African Americans. They also ran the local economy.

Pirates of Somalia capture large ships. The owners of these ships pay millions of dollars to get them back. Other governments have to send in troops to stop the pirates of Somalia.

Fighting for an Oligarchy

By 1840, almost every black person was a slave in many places in the South. The few men that owned the large farms made sure that everything stayed the same. They also controlled citizens who were not slaves. These poor people ended up fighting and dying in the Civil War. They fought for the few men who kept them poor.

Almost no one from the oligarchy fought in the war. They helped pass a law that protected them. Their families could keep one man out of the army for every 20 slaves they owned. Many wealthy families lost their plantations during the war. However, of the 25 most powerful oligarchs, 18 were still going strong after the war.

Modern Pirates

In Africa, Somalia lacks a strong central government. It does not have a navy or coast guard. This situation has allowed local oligarchies of pirates to take control of many areas along the coast. Pirate ships attack ships in the Indian Ocean. They then hold the ships and people hostage for **ransoms**. The pirate oligarchs claim they are trying to stop illegal fishing and keep other nations from dumping toxic waste off the Somali coastline. But in reality, they make millions of dollars from piracy.

In some countries, the police and the courts do not enforce the laws. Oligarchies have to protect themselves in these countries. Many of them hire their own armies. Others make sure that they can control the army of their country.

But most oligarchies have less to fear from armies attacking their holdings. Their real enemy is an army of tax collectors.

Defending Great Wealth

Oligarchs can afford to hire the finest minds. They seek out people who have worked with the government. They hire former tax collectors. These people know how to hide wealth. They have worked for the agencies that try to tax the elites. Highly skilled lawyers create trusts or estates for them. A trust is a legal arrangement. Wealth is set aside for children to use later in life. Having an estate controls taxes after death. Both of these are used to keep money in a family.

Oligarchs also hire the best bankers, **accountants**, and other experts. They show oligarchs how to use their wealth in **investments** such as real estate. They may also buy parts of companies. Investments can be loans to businesses as well. Elites put their money to work this way to avoid taxes.

The tax laws in the United States are very complex. They allow people to pay fewer taxes if they use their money in certain ways. Most oligarchs take advantage of these tax breaks.

Oligarchies also try to control the laws through **lobbyists**. These people try to get politicians to pass laws that favor the elite. Some people even hide their money. They put it in foreign countries so they do not pay any taxes on it.

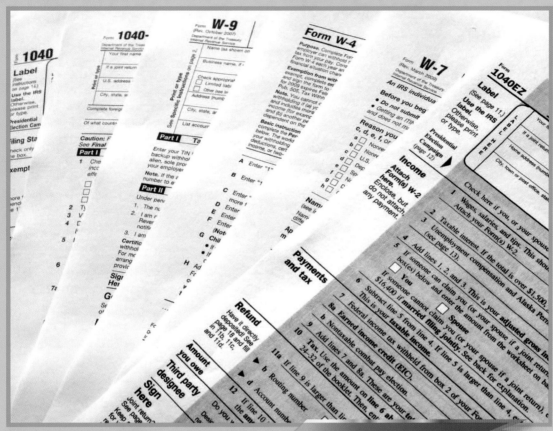

Most oligarchs feel that they pay too much in taxes. This is because they pay large amounts. But they also earn enormous incomes. They usually pay only a small portion of their profits in taxes.

Not a Fair Fight

All of this is perfectly legal. There is no crime in finding ways within the law to pay fewer taxes. The oligarchs will win in the end. It costs the government huge sums to collect taxes. Tax collectors do not have armies of experts like those used by wealthy oligarchs who legally avoid taxes. The elites also spend larger amounts on purchases than most people. Yet they are allowed to subtract those costs from their taxes, which most people cannot do.

The First Tax on Oligarchs

For most of U.S. history, there were no income taxes. Income is the amount of money someone is paid for work. In 1884, Congress passed a bill to tax only the wealthiest citizens. They, of course, fought this. Most refused to pay. By 1913, everyone had to pay income tax. Of course, the oligarchs were soon paying much less. Everyone else paid more of their income to the government.

Some oligarchies become very powerful on their own. They never become part of the government. Oligarchs in business can grow so large that they are like a government all by themselves.

Robber Baron Oligarchs

The greatest oligarchy in America began after the Civil War ended in 1865. A few people made fortunes fast. New railroads, cheap natural resources, and factories made some people rich like never before. But a few of those people wanted to be more than wealthy. They realized they could take over certain industries. They could make almost every penny to be had. They were called the robber barons. They attempted to create **monopolies**. They wanted complete control of an industry. Then they would be more powerful than the government. Together, they would be the government.

Rockefeller and Oil

One famous robber baron was John D. Rockefeller. He took over the oil industry. Rockefeller made a secret deal with the railroad robber barons. This forced everyone out of the oil business. He then controlled all the pipelines. He also bought up all the places that sold oil.

Other robber barons controlled other industries. Andrew Carnegie bought up all the U.S. steel companies. J.P. Morgan owned the banks. Jay Gould almost controlled all the gold. The wealth of these men allowed them to become another government besides the national one. They controlled prices and formed trusts. A trust is a group of companies formed to control the making and distributing of a product. These trusts allowed oligarchs complete control over many industries in the country.

One of the wealthiest men in the United States, John D. Rockefeller often gave out dimes. Through corrupt control of industries, robber barons like Rockefeller kept their power and wealth for decades.

Owned by Rockefeller and his partners, the Standard Oil Company controlled almost all the production, processing, and shipping of oil in the United States.

The Trust Busters

The U.S. government was finally forced to take action. Congress passed the Sherman Antitrust Act in 1890. The courts supported this law. The robber barons were forced to sell off many of their companies. They were divided into smaller companies. This way, more owners would compete against each other. One owner could not control entire industries. The government also began to control prices. It also kept trusts from starting up.

Corporate Oligarchies

John D. Rockefeller also created the first corporation. Many people owned the corporation and invested their money in it. This company or group of people can act as a single unit. Rockefeller could not be blamed for what his corporation did. Of course, Rockefeller and other oligarchs owned at least 51 percent of it. That way, it would have to do what they wanted. And he could still claim it was not an illegal trust.

OLIGARCHIES TODAY

Many of the wealthiest and most powerful countries today are oligarchies. Yet they do not openly admit it. And because these oligarchies are still in power, it is difficult to prove they exist.

Modern oligarchs come from all over the world. They dominate the world economy. They gather in places that protect their wealth, such as the city-state of Singapore.

Billionaires and Millionaires

Singapore is a tiny city-state in Asia. Large numbers of oligarchs from other countries have gathered there. Of its five million residents, 11 are billionaires. They own five percent of all the wealth in the world. There are also 100,000 millionaires. They control 50 percent of the wealth in this well-to-do nation. These oligarchs allow other officials to rule the nation.

Return to Russian Oligarchy

Russian communism failed in the late 1980s. Elected governments grew in its place. But suddenly there was an explosion of oligarchs. In the past, most Russians could not gain great wealth. The sources of wealth were owned by the country itself, not individual millionaires. Only the Communist Party elite became very wealthy. In recent years, without the Communist Party to control the economy, a new class of oligarchs appeared. Through government connections and secret contracts, they took control of all the oil, coal, and steel. The government has tried to control them. Yet it was the government that made many of them very wealthy.

China today has the world's fastest growing economy. Cheap labor, its secret government's strong control, and wealthy oligarchs make that growth possible.

Chinese Communist Millionaires

China today also fits the definition of a modern oligarchy. China has been under the control of the Communist Party since World War II. However, a central committee of the party really controls everything. A small group of oligarchs control this committee. They take care of themselves first. In the past, their mistakes have caused millions of Chinese to starve to death. But over the last few decades, China has changed rapidly. It has allowed a small group of Chinese millionaires to gain great wealth. They use low-paid workers to make things cheaply in China. The government has benefited from the money these millionaires bring into the country. But the Communist Party is still in charge. It is one oligarchy controlling another oligarchy.

Is India an Oligarchy?

Russia has more than 87 billionaires. This is the most of any country. But India, a very poor country, has 55 billionaires. This is more than Brazil and Germany, which are very rich countries. They only have 18 each. Both India's and Russia's billionaires got rich the same way. They seized their country's natural resources. They took public land and government contracts away from their people.

Media Oligarchies

Many experts feel that the United States is controlled by a rich and powerful oligarchy. They point to the fact that most of the wealth in this country is held by a small number of people. They note that only a few large banks control the money flow. They argue that a wealthy elite influences government officials to do what they want. Most of all they can easily show that an oligarchy rules the media in America today.

Six U.S. Media Oligarchs

All oligarchies are, by their nature, secret. An oligarchy in power does not want people to know it is controlling the government. No one has been able to prove that the media oligarchs work together. Yet there is no denying that they determine what most people in this country watch or hear. Six major companies own almost all the television and radio stations, cable outlets, newspapers, and Internet services. This is a recent change. Thirty years ago, more than 50 corporations owned the media.

International Media Oligarchs

This same power of a few media owners is seen around the world. In Australia, two companies control most of the newspapers. A small number of companies own most of the media in Canada. Swiss and German corporations possess most media in the Czech Republic. One giant German media concern owns hundreds of newspapers across Europe and other media in North America. Individuals or their families control most of the media of Italy and Great Britain. Two companies own all the television and radio stations in Mexico. In China, the government has allowed private companies to own some of the state media. However, it still heavily **censors** any media, including the Internet, inside of China.

In the past, oligarchs defended their wealth with armies and secret police. Today they tend to own the sources of information through the media. This keeps them out of the spotlight and still in power.

The oligarchs who control the media make fortunes. They may show off their wealth with luxury yachts. Their real power, however, is keeping the average person from understanding the effect they have on the flow of information.

The oligarchies in North Korea and Syria control all media. In China and some Arab countries, the elites only restrict parts of the media. What they like is not banned. Any criticism directed at the oligarchs is censored.

A free and open media has become increasingly important. People today rely more and more on television, radio, and the Internet for their news. Many governments have appointed groups to study the effects of their media being owned and controlled by only a few parties. In the past, oligarchies relied on armies and their control of wealth. Today, those few who control the media, control information. The media has become a new tool for the oligarchs.

An American Money Oligarchy

Only 400 taxpayers own two percent of all the money in the United States. Two percent may not sound like much, but it means they averaged about $350 million each in yearly income. The next 15,000 individuals own six percent of America's wealth. And the top 10 percent of the wealthy own half of all the money. That means only 135,000 people in a country of more than 300 million people own half the wealth.

FORMS OF GOVERNMENT

	Democracy	Dictatorship
Basis of power	People elect officials to represent their views and beliefs.	The dictator controls everything in the country. His word is the law.
Rights of the people	People have many rights, including the right to fair and free elections, the right to assemble, and the right to choose how to live their lives.	The people have very few rights. Their duty is to do whatever the dictator wants.
How leaders are chosen	Frequent and regular elections are held to vote for leaders.	Leaders can inherit their position or take it with military force. The most powerful political party may also choose them.
Basis of judicial branch	A separate judicial branch enforces the laws made by the legislative branch. Laws are supposed to be enforced freely and fairly.	The judicial branch does what the dictator wants.
Relation of business to the form of government	Government plays a limited role in businesses. They may charge taxes and make some laws to make sure businesses are run fairly.	The government often owns the major businesses in a country.
Control of media	The government does not control the media. People have access to many opinions and diverse information from the media.	The dictator either tells the media what to report or censors the media's reports.
Role of religion	People may choose to practice their own religion.	People may or may not be able to practice their religion freely. However, political parties and focus on the dictator's personality are more important than religion.

Monarchy	Oligarchy	Theocracy
A monarch's power is inherited from a previous **generation.** In absolute monarchies, monarchs are believed to be chosen by God.	A select few use their wealth or secret connections to powerful people in the government to control the country. They are rarely elected.	The government is based on the state religion.
Rights are not guaranteed in an **absolute monarchy.** In a **constitutional monarchy**, rights are outlined in the country's constitution.	No rights are guaranteed, but in elected oligarchies, citizens can vote.	The laws of the state religion limit the rights of the people.
Power is passed down through families. Monarchies have different rules for who inherits power. In constitutional monarchies, the leaders of governing bodies, such as a parliament, are chosen through elections.	Oligarchs take power in most cases. They are rarely elected. They usually lead hidden behind the government.	Leaders are elected or appointed or chosen by religious customs.
In absolute monarchies, monarchs run the courts. Most constitutional monarchies have a separate judicial branch to ensure fair treatment.	Most oligarchies hide behind regular government functions. With their money and power, they affect the judicial branch's decisions.	All laws are based on the state religion. The judicial branch bases its judgments on that religion's laws.
Leaders of absolute monarchies control all of the wealth of a country. In constitutional monarchies, decisions about business are made by a governing body, such as a parliament.	Many oligarchs control wealthy businesses.	Businesses can be owned by citizens or by the government.
The press is not free in an absolute monarchy. Many constitutional monarchies, however, guarantee freedom of the media and speech.	Oligarchs tend to own and control all the media.	The media can be controlled by the government or by private citizens. It must follow the laws of the state religion.
Absolute monarchies often require people to have the same religion as the monarch. Many constitutional monarchies guarantee freedom of religion.	Some oligarchs share a common religion.	Religion forms the basis of the government. It dictates most aspects of the citizens' lives.

Most oligarchies choose the country they want to control. Sometimes countries lack a central leader, and oligarchies fill the gap. Oligarchies can also come to power through the collapse of a government.

Oligarchs with wealth and property have something to lose. They act to protect their interests. They may create a committee or a secret group to keep others from taking away what they have.

The Benefits of Oligarchy

An oligarchy makes sure that the parts of the economy it controls are healthy. A successful oligarchy tries to make sure that the government is stable. Most people have jobs, which helps average citizens. People make money. This benefit is seen in Singapore. Average incomes are high there.

Oligarchies can also help maintain order. Their power keeps different elements of society from fighting with each other. This may mean that some parts of society suffer. But those who support the oligarchy benefit. For example, whites in South Africa lived a good life during the era of apartheid. Being part of that oligarchy benefited them but hurt most Africans.

Russian oligarch Roman Abramovich watches one of the soccer teams he owns. Oligarchs often try to do things, such as promoting sports, to please ordinary citizens.

The Drawbacks of Oligarchy

The order that oligarchies bring can also be a bad thing. In Indonesia and Guatemala, oligarchies took most of the money and resources. They gave little back to the citizens. So, even though there was order and money, few people enjoyed it. These oligarchies are harmful to their countries' population.

Oligarchies object to change because it might take away their power and wealth. During the 1500s, Spain took over most of Central and South America. In 1812, France attacked Spain in Europe. Spain lost control of these colonies. The people in Central and South America rejoiced. They thought they would get their independence from Spain.

In Mexico, Father Miguel Hidalgo y Costilla led a revolution. In 1810, he and others formed an army of 80,000 peasants and Native Americans. They could easily have taken Mexico City. But the poor people were so angry they destroyed everything they conquered. This violence kept the rest of the country from joining them.

Hiding behind the Spanish government were powerful oligarchies in Mexico and the other colonies. They quickly crushed any ideas of freedom for the people. They replaced Spain as the central power. The oligarchies needed order. They had to protect their wealth. They were not about to let the people be free.

A Catholic priest named Father Hidalgo failed to overthrow the Spanish oligarchs in Mexico. Today he is a national hero.

An Oligarchy Creates a Country

In 1788, Great Britain sent its criminals away to Australia. Men and women were put in prisons controlled by guards and a small government. The guards and government soon became an oligarchy. They ran the country and made money off the prisoners. But in time, the prisoners were freed. They soon became citizens of Australia. The elites lost control. In the end, Australia became a great democracy.

When a small group of people gains power, they create an oligarchy. They use their wealth to control a society. Few oligarchies use the powers they have for the good of their people. However, if they are wise, they try to spread their wealth. Many different parts of society can benefit from their power. They can produce success for many more than just a privileged few.

Oligarchies in a Stable Country

The Scandinavian countries of northern Europe are a good example. Their governments are strong. There is little poverty. Most of the population has a comfortable living. Surprisingly, there are a relatively high number of oligarchs. The wealthy few can still have their wealth because the rest of the country is also benefiting. The elites are sharing their success. The country is better off for it.

A Failing Oligarchy

Since 1954, the government of Egypt has been elected by the people. Yet it has been little more than an oligarchy. The owners of the nation's industries run the country. They are also the heads of the government. These few have monopolies on steel, automobiles, cement, and even food. They are called The Whales because they take so much. Egypt has remained poor. The Arab Spring uprising came in early 2011. It removed President Hosni Mubarak, who had gathered great wealth during his 30 years in power. However, the economy is still controlled by an oligarchy.

A mass movement such as Egypt's Arab Spring uprising can make changes. However, in Egypt, only the ruler changed, and the oligarchies remained.

Oligarchies can remain in power through a variety of methods. In Argentina, the ruling elite has kept power through strong labor unions. These groups of workers join together to protect their wages, benefits, and working conditions.

Elected Oligarchies

Oligarchies exist even in countries where most of the citizens are doing well. These voters actually chose to keep their oligarchies in place. They appear to believe oligarchies work for them.

Argentina is an example of this type of oligarchy. Voters have continued to re-elect one political party. This party is controlled by a group of elites. Long ago, these same elites took over after Argentina gained independence from Spain. Today they still tightly control the country's wealth. The oligarchy remains because the people are satisfied.

Defeating an Oligarchy

The first English colony in America was Jamestown. It was controlled by an elite group from the Virginia Company. They wanted the settlers to dig for gold. There was no gold, and the settlers began to starve. John Smith led a revolution. He forced the elites to give everyone land. Soon the colony had farms and food. Sometimes the people have to force the oligarchy to give them what they need.

Before 1994, a small population of white colonists ruled over millions of native Africans in South Africa. In 1948, the ruling National Party issued the following statement to justify their policy of apartheid.

"There are two sections of thought in South Africa in regard to the policy affecting the non-European community. On the one hand there is the policy of equality, which advocates equal rights within the same political structure for all civilized and educated persons, **irrespective** of race or colour, and the gradual granting of the **franchise** to non-Europeans as they become qualified to make use of democratic rights.

"On the other hand there is the policy of separation (apartheid) which has grown from the experience of established European population of the country, and which is based on the Christian principles of Justice and reasonableness.

"Its aim is the maintenance and protection of the European population of the country as a pure White race, the maintenance and protection of the **indigenous** racial groups as separate communities...

In 1990, the president of South Africa, Frederik de Klerk, and Nelson Mandela, the leader of the African National Congress, brought an end to the practice of apartheid.

"We can act in only, one of two directions. Either we must follow the course of equality, which must eventually mean national suicide for the White race, or we must take the course of separation (apartheid) through which the character and the future of every race will be protected and safeguarded with full opportunities for development and self-maintenance in their own ideas, without the interests of one clashing with the interests of the other, and without one regarding the development of the other as undermining or a threat to himself.

"The party therefore undertakes to protect the White race properly and effectively against any policy, doctrine or attack which might undermine or threaten its continued existence..."

Plato's *Republic*

The ancient Greek philosopher Plato outlined several forms of government in his political and social book *Republic*. He gives his thinking in the form of discussions among two or more people.

Book VIII

"This, then, will be the first great defect of oligarchy?"

"Clearly."

"And here is another defect which is quite as bad."

"What defect?"

"The inevitable division: such a State is not one, but two States, the one of poor, the other of rich men; and they are living on the same spot and always conspiring against one another."

The Greek philosopher Plato warned early on that the danger of oligarchies was their control of a country's wealth.

"That, surely, is at least as bad."

"...for a like reason, they are incapable of carrying on any war. Either they arm the multitude, and then they are more afraid of them than of the enemy; or, if they do not call them out in the hour of battle, they are oligarchs indeed, few to fight as they are few to rule. And at the same time their fondness for money makes them unwilling to pay taxes."

GLOSSARY

absolute monarchy A government in which a ruler controls every aspect of government. Rule is passed along family lines.

accountants People trained to take care of the money records of a person or business

apartheid A policy of separating people according to race or other factor

aristocrats A group of individuals who are born into a high social position

barons Noblemen of the lowest rank

Bolshevik Someone belonging to the Communist Party that seized power in Russia in November 1917

bureaucracy A group of unelected officials that run an organization

capital The total amount of property or money owned by a person or business

censors Prevents publication of or removes ideas that go against the government's views and goals

city-state An area, made up of a city and its surrounding region, that governs itself

class A group or rank of society. Lower classes typically have less money than upper classes.

Communist A system of government in which a single party controls all businesses and agriculture. Under Communism, all property is supposed to be publicly owned, and people work and are paid according to their abilities.

conquistadors Leaders in the Spanish conquest of the Americas during the 1500s

constitutional monarchy A system of government in which a king, queen, or sultan shares power, usually with an elected government.

corrupt Willing to be dishonest in exchange for money or personal gain

descendants People who come from a particular ancestor or group of ancestors

dictator A leader who has absolute power over a country

dictatorships Systems of government in which the leader of a country has absolute power

elite Groups of people thought to be the best in a specific society or activity because of their power, talent, or wealth

empires A group of countries under the rule of one leader

equivalent Equal or alike in value, number, or meaning

feudal system Political arrangement during the Middle Ages in western Europe. Under the feudal system, a lord provided land and protection for people under his rule, and in return, they promised service and loyalty to the lord.

feuds Bitter, long-lasting, violent arguments between two people, families, or groups

fleet A group of ships

franchise The right to vote

generation Individuals who are one step in the line of descent of a family. A grandmother, mother, and daughter are three generations of a family.

guilds A group of people with the same craft; an organization of people with the same interests or goals

indigenous Describes something produced or living naturally in a particular region

investments Companies, lands, or items that are bought with the hope that they will be worth more money in the future than the purchase price

irrespective Without regard to

lobbyists People who are paid to persuade government leaders to vote a certain way

monarchies Forms of government in which one person rules for life

monopolies Complete control of products or services by one person or company

Parliament A group of people who have the duty and power to make the laws of a country

philosopher Someone who studies the basic nature and purpose of life, the universe, and truth

plutocracy Government by the wealthy

ransoms The money paid or demanded before a captive is set free

Renaissance The period of European history from the 1300s to the 1600s marked by an increased interest in art and literature inspired by ancient times and by the beginnings of modern science

reserves Areas of land set apart for peoples

theocracies Governments in which the people who run the government belong to a specific religion

warlord A leader who governs an area by force

World War II A war fought from 1939 to 1945 in which the United Kingdom, the United States, France, Russia, China, and other countries defeated Germany, Italy, and Japan

FOR MORE INFORMATION

Books

Apel, Melanie Ann. *Politics and Government in Ancient Greece*, Primary Sources of Ancient Civilization: Greece. New York: PowerKids Press, 2004.

Gedacht, Daniel C. *Politics and Government in Ancient Rome*, Primary Sources of Ancient Civilization: Rome. New York: Rosen Publishing, 2004.

Giesecke, Ernestine. *Governments Around the World*, Kids' Guide to Government. Chicago: Heinemann Library, 2009.

Hunt, Jilly. *Russia*, Countries Around the World. Chicago: Heinemann Library, 2012.

Layton, Lesley. *Singapore*, Cultures of the World. New York: Marshall Cavendish Benchmark Books, 2012

Wagner, Heather Lehr. *The Medicis: A Ruling Dynasty*, Makers of the Middle Ages and Renaissance. Philadelphia: Chelsea House Publishers, 2005.

Websites

Academic Kids: academickids.com/encyclopedia/index.php/Oligarchy

Kidipede: www.historyforkids.org/learn/government/oligarchy.htm

Life 123: www.life123.com/parenting/education/social-studies/oligarchy-facts.shtml

INDEX